That Tyrannosaurus rex skeleton is so cool! What? You wish you could see a T. rex alive? You know a T. rex could bite through a car, right? And you still really want to meet a living Tyrannosaurus rex?

Well, then you'll need a time machine. Go back 67 million years to the Cretaceous Period, before dinosaurs went extinct. That's before your great-great-great-great-great-grandparents were born. In fact, it's millions of years before any humans lived!

Where should you go? Lots of T. rex fossils have been discovered along the border of Montana and South Dakota. Head there.

You won't need a jacket. But pull on rubber boots. It's hot and swampy here in the time of dinosaurs.

Is that a T. rex? No, this dinosaur is munching on leaves. It's a hadrosaur! They have duck bills. T. rex is a carnivore and only eats meat.

Here's a huge footprint with three large toes. That matches the T. rex bones in the museum. Maybe there are more footprints.

Don't look too near for the next footprint. T. rex could cover about 6 feet (2 m) in one step! So you'll take about four steps for every T. rex step.

There it is! T. rex stretches as long as three cars—about 40 feet (12 m). And it stands 15 feet (4.6 m) tall—that's about as tall as three sixth graders on each other's shoulders!

Uh-oh. Is the T. rex looking your way? T. rex has excellent eyesight, which helps it find prey. And you're snack size! Hold still. Maybe it won't see you.

Look at those nostrils! T. rex can smell even better than it sees. You did take a bath this morning, didn't you?

Whew! It's after the hadrosaur, not you. T. rex doesn't grab prey with its arms. It just bites down on whatever it's chasing. Even an alligator bite would feel gentle next to a T. rex bite. Chomp!

The hadrosaur got away. Looks like T. rex lost a tooth while trying to bite it. Don't worry. T. rex still has 57 more big teeth. Each tooth is the size of a banana! And pretty soon a new tooth will grow in.

T. rex has found the carcass of a dead dinosaur. If it can't get live prey, T. rex scavenges, eating the meat off dead animals it finds.

Is it looking at you again? Get back to the time machine. Double quick!

Seeing a T. rex up close is cool. But it wouldn't be so cool to be inside one!

WHERE HAVE TYRANNOSAURUS REX FOSSILS BEEN FOUND?

GLOSSARY

carcass—The dead body of an animal.

carnivore—An animal that eats only meat.

Cretaceous Period—The time between 145.5 million and 65.5 million years ago. Dinosaurs lived during this time.

extinct—No longer found living anywhere in the world; known only from fossils.

fossil—A bone or other trace of an animal from millions of years ago, preserved as rock.

hadrosaur—A duck-billed, plant-eating dinosaur.

prey—An animal hunted and killed for food by another animal.

scavenge—To search for and eat dead animals.

AUTHOR'S NOTE

Too bad for us, time machines aren't real. But all of the details about the T. rex in this book are based on research by scientists who study fossils. For example, in 2013 scientists announced they had found a T. rex tooth deep in the bones of a hadrosaur tail. This clue suggests that T. rex was a hunter but that sometimes its prey escaped! New dinosaur discoveries are made every year. Look up the books and websites below to learn more.

READ MORE

Holtz, Thomas R. *Digging for Tyrannosaurus rex*. North Mankato, Minn.: Capstone Press, 2015.

Sabatino, Michael. *T. rex vs. Crocodile*. New York: Gareth Stevens Publishing, 2016.

Stewart, Melissa. *Why Did T. rex Have Short Arms? And Other Questions about Dinosaurs*. New York: Sterling Children's Books, 2014.

WEBSITES

BEYOND T. REX: AMERICAN MUSEUM OF NATURAL HISTORY OLOGY
http://www.amnh.org/explore/ology/ paleontology/beyond-t.-rex
Play a game to learn more about T. rex and his relatives.

SUE THE T. REX: THE FIELD MUSEUM
https://www.fieldmuseum.org/at-the-field/ exhibitions/sue-t-rex
"Sue" is one of the largest T. rex skeletons ever found. Explore the website for photo galleries, videos, and more.

Every effort has been made to ensure that these websites are appropriate for children. However, because of the nature of the Internet, it is impossible to guarantee that these sites will remain active indefinitely or that their contents will not be altered.